A GIFT FOR:

_____

FROM:

_____

DAILY CALM

Photos and Wisdom to Soothe Your Spirit

NATIONAL GEOGRAPHIC

WASHINGTON, D.C.

ISBN: 978-1-59530-728-6
BOK2190

Made in China

DAILY CALM

You cannot travel on the Path
before you have become
that Path itself.

~ BUDDHA

*We must go ahead
and see for ourselves.*

~ JACQUES COUSTEAU

Day 3

If there is no struggle,
there is no progress.

~ Frederick Douglass

Faith is taking the first step even when you don't see the whole staircase.

~ MARTIN LUTHER KING, JR.

One doesn't discover new lands
without consenting to lose sight of
the shore for a very long time.

~ ANDRÉ GIDE

All change is a miracle to contemplate, but it is a miracle which is taking place every instant.

~ HENRY DAVID THOREAU

*In three words, I can sum up
everything I've learned about life:
it goes on.*

~ Robert Frost

DAY 8

Dead my old fine hopes
And dry my dreaming, but oh . . .
Iris, blue each spring!

~ SHUSHIKI

Your hand opens and closes, opens and closes.
If it were always a fist or always stretched open,
you would be paralyzed.

~ RUMI

DAY 10

We are not yet what we shall be, but we are growing toward it, the process is not yet finished . . .

~ MARTIN LUTHER

There will come a time when
you believe everything is finished.
That will be the beginning.

~ LOUIS L'AMOUR

*A merry heart doeth good
like a medicine.*

~ PROVERBS 17:22

DAY 13

The moment of change
is the only poem.

~ ADRIENNE RICH

*Disconnecting from change
does not recapture the past.
It loses the future.*

~ Kathleen Norris

Kiss, n. *A word invented by the poets*
as a rhyme for "bliss."

~ AMBROSE BIERCE

He who bends to himself a Joy
Doth the winged life destroy;
But he who kisses the Joy as it flies
Lives in Eternity's sunrise.

~ WILLIAM BLAKE

Rapidly, merrily,
Life's sunny hours flit by,
Gratefully, cheerily,
Enjoy them as they fly!

~ CHARLOTTE BRONTË

*To be in love is to touch things
with a lighter hand.*

~ GWENDOLYN BROOKS

DAY 19

There is no pleasure in having
nothing to do; the fun is in having
lots to do—and not doing it.

~ MARY LITTLE

DAY 20

Growth and self-transformation
cannot be delegated.

~ LEWIS MUMFORD

*One cannot divine nor forecast the conditions that
will make happiness; one only
stumbles upon them by chance, in a lucky hour,
at the world's end somewhere, and holds fast to
the days, as to fortune or fame.*

~ WILLA CATHER

DAY 22

With mirth and laughter let old wrinkles come.

~ WILLIAM SHAKESPEARE

*What we lack is not so much
leisure to do as time to reflect
and time to feel.*

~ MARGARET MEAD

The easiest way to avoid wrong notes is to never open your mouth and sing. What a mistake that would be.

~ Joan Oliver Goldsmith

*Every beginning
is only a sequel, after all,
and the book of events
is always open halfway through.*

~ WISŁAWA SZYMBORSKA

*We ought not to look back,
unless it is to derive useful lessons
from past errors.*

~ GEORGE WASHINGTON

Mistakes are part of the dues one pays
for living a full life.

~ SOPHIA LOREN

The man who has lived most is not he who has numbered the most years, but he who has had the keenest sense of life.

~ JEAN-JACQUES ROUSSEAU

In youth we learn, in age we understand.

~ MARIE VON EBNER-ESCHENBACH

*You practice and you get better.
It's very simple.*

~ PHILIP GLASS

Adventure is something you seek for pleasure, or even for profit . . . but experience is what really happens to you in the long run; the truth that finally overtakes you.

~ Katherine Anne Porter

Education is when you read the fine print.
Experience is what you get if you don't.

~ PETE SEEGER

DAY 33

*It is the sweet, simple things of life
which are the real ones after all.*

~ LAURA INGALLS WILDER

Don't eat anything your great-grandmother
wouldn't recognize as food.

~ MICHAEL POLLAN

*To find the air and the water exhilarating;
to be refreshed by a morning walk or an evening saunter;
to be thrilled by the stars at night; to be elated over
a bird's nest, or over a wild flower in spring—
these are some of the rewards of the simple life.*

~ John Burroughs

The wisdom of life consists in the elimination of non-essentials.

~ LIN YUTANG

The art of art, the glory of expression and the sunshine of the light of letters, is simplicity.

~ WALT WHITMAN

*Simplify the problem of life: distinguish
the necessary and the real. Probe the earth
to see where your main roots run.*

~ HENRY DAVID THOREAU

*Silence is more musical
than any song.*

~ CHRISTINA ROSSETTI

As I grew older, I realized that it was much better to insist on the genuine forms of nature, for simplicity is the greatest adornment of art.

~ ALBRECHT DÜRER

I adore simple pleasures.
They are the last refuge of the complex.

~ OSCAR WILDE

Broadly speaking,
short words are best,
and the old words, when short,
are best of all.

~ WINSTON CHURCHILL

*Have nothing in
your house that you
do not know to be
useful, or believe to be
beautiful.*

~ WILLIAM MORRIS

Be good, keep your feet dry, your eyes open,
your heart at peace . . .

~ THOMAS MERTON

Omit needless words.

~ WILLIAM STRUNK AND E. B. WHITE

To me a lush carpet of pine needles or spongy grass is more welcome than the most luxurious Persian rug.

~ HELEN KELLER

It is only when we are aware of the earth and of the earth as poetry that we truly live.

~ HENRY BESTON

*Reduce the complexity of life
by eliminating the needless
wants of life, and the labors
of life reduce themselves.*

—EDWIN WAY TEALE

Simplicity is an exact medium
between too little and too much.

~ SIR JOSHUA REYNOLDS

DAY 50

Rain is grace; rain is the sky
condescending to the earth;
without rain, there would be no life.

~ JOHN UPDIKE

*Very little is needed to
make a happy life.*

~ Marcus Aurelius

The smell of good bread baking,
like the sound of lightly flowing water,
is indescribable in its evocation of
innocence and delight.

~ M. F. K. FISHER

Learn to wish that everything
may happen as it does.

~ EPICTETUS

Believe that you have it,
and you have it.

~ LATIN PROVERB

*Little by little, through patience
and repeated effort, the mind will
become stilled in the Self.*

~ HINDU SCRIPTURE

Learn to be quiet enough to hear the sound of the genuine within yourself, so that you can hear it in other people.

~ MARIAN WRIGHT EDELMAN

*. . . those who do not observe the movements of
their own minds must of necessity be unhappy.*

~ MARCUS AURELIUS

Our true nature is not some deal that we have to live up to. It's who we are right now, and that's what we can make friends with and celebrate.

~ PEMA CHÖDRÖN

Remember, remember,
this is now, and now, and now.
Live it, feel it, cling to it.

~ SYLVIA PLATH

Strange as it may seem today to say, the aim of life is to live, and to live means to be aware, joyously, drunkenly, serenely, divinely aware.

~ HENRY MILLER

The breeze of grace is always blowing on you,
but you have to unfurl your sails.

~ SRI RAMAKRISHNA

DAY 62

*Of many magics, one is watching
a beloved sleep: free of eyes and
awareness, you for a sweet moment
hold the heart of him.*

~ TRUMAN CAPOTE

Who looks outside, dreams;
who looks inside, awakes.

~ Carl Jung

Breathe-in experience,
breathe-out poetry.

~ MURIEL RUKEYSER

No longer forward or behind
I look in hope or fear;
But, grateful, take the good I find,
The best of now and here.

~ JOHN GREENLEAF WHITTIER

You certainly usually find something,
if you look, but it is not always quite
the something you were after.

~ J. R. R. TOLKIEN

Each situation—
nay, each moment—
is of infinite worth;
for each represents
a whole eternity.

~ Johann Wolfgang von Goethe

One's life has value only so long as one attributes value to the lives of others by means of love, friendship, indignation, compassion.

~ Simone de Beauvoir

What do we live for, if it is not to make
life less difficult for each other?

~ GEORGE ELIOT

For those to whom much is given, much is required.

~ JOHN F. KENNEDY

Constant kindness can accomplish much.
As the sun makes ice melt, kindness causes
misunderstanding, mistrust,
and hostility to evaporate.

~ ALBERT SCHWEITZER

DAY 72

Only if we understand, can we care.
Only if we care, will we help.
Only if we help, shall all be saved.

~ JANE GOODALL

DAY 73

There is no charm equal to
tenderness of heart.

~ JANE AUSTEN

*With malice toward none,
with charity for all.*

~ ABRAHAM LINCOLN

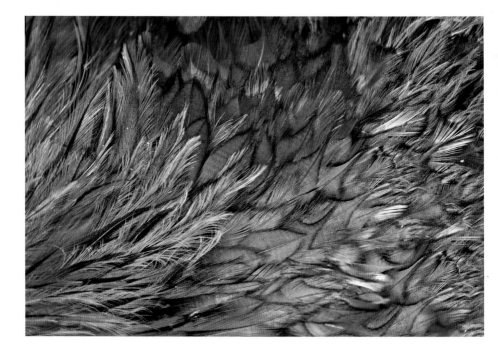

The softest thing in the universe
overcomes the hardest.

~ LAO-TZU

The more one judges,
the less one loves.

~ HONORÉ DE BALZAC

DAY 77

*He who sows courtesy
reaps friendship,
and he who plants
kindness gathers love.*

~ PROVERB

One kind word can warm
three winter months.

~ JAPANESE PROVERB

Carry out a random act of kindness, with no expectation of reward, safe in the knowledge that one day someone might do the same for you.

~ DIANA, PRINCESS OF WALES

Have a heart that never hardens,
and a temper that never tires,
and a touch that never hurts.

~ CHARLES DICKENS

Love doesn't just sit there, like a stone,
it has to be made, like bread;
re-made all the time, made new.

~ URSULA K. LE GUIN

*The giving of love is an
education in itself.*

~ ELEANOR ROOSEVELT

From what we get, we can make a living;
what we give, however, makes a life.

~ ARTHUR ASHE

*If the doors of perception were cleansed,
everything would appear to man
as it is, infinite.*

~ WILLIAM BLAKE

*The greatest good you can do for
another is not just to share your riches
but to reveal to him his own.*

~ BENJAMIN DISRAELI

I want to stay as close to the edge as I can without going over. Out on the edge you can see all kinds of things you can't see from the center.

~ KURT VONNEGUT

I think we find happiness in retrospect.
We don't recognize it in the moment.

~ EVELYN CUNNINGHAM

DAY 88

For us believing physicists,
the distinction between past, present,
and future is only an illusion,
even if a stubborn one.

~ ALBERT EINSTEIN

We all live in suspense, from day to day,
from hour to hour; in other words,
we are the hero of our own story.

~ MARY McCARTHY

The locus of the human mystery
is perception of this world.
From it proceeds every thought,
every art.

~ MARILYNNE ROBINSON

Day 91

We are all in the gutter,
but some of us are looking
at the stars.

~ Oscar Wilde

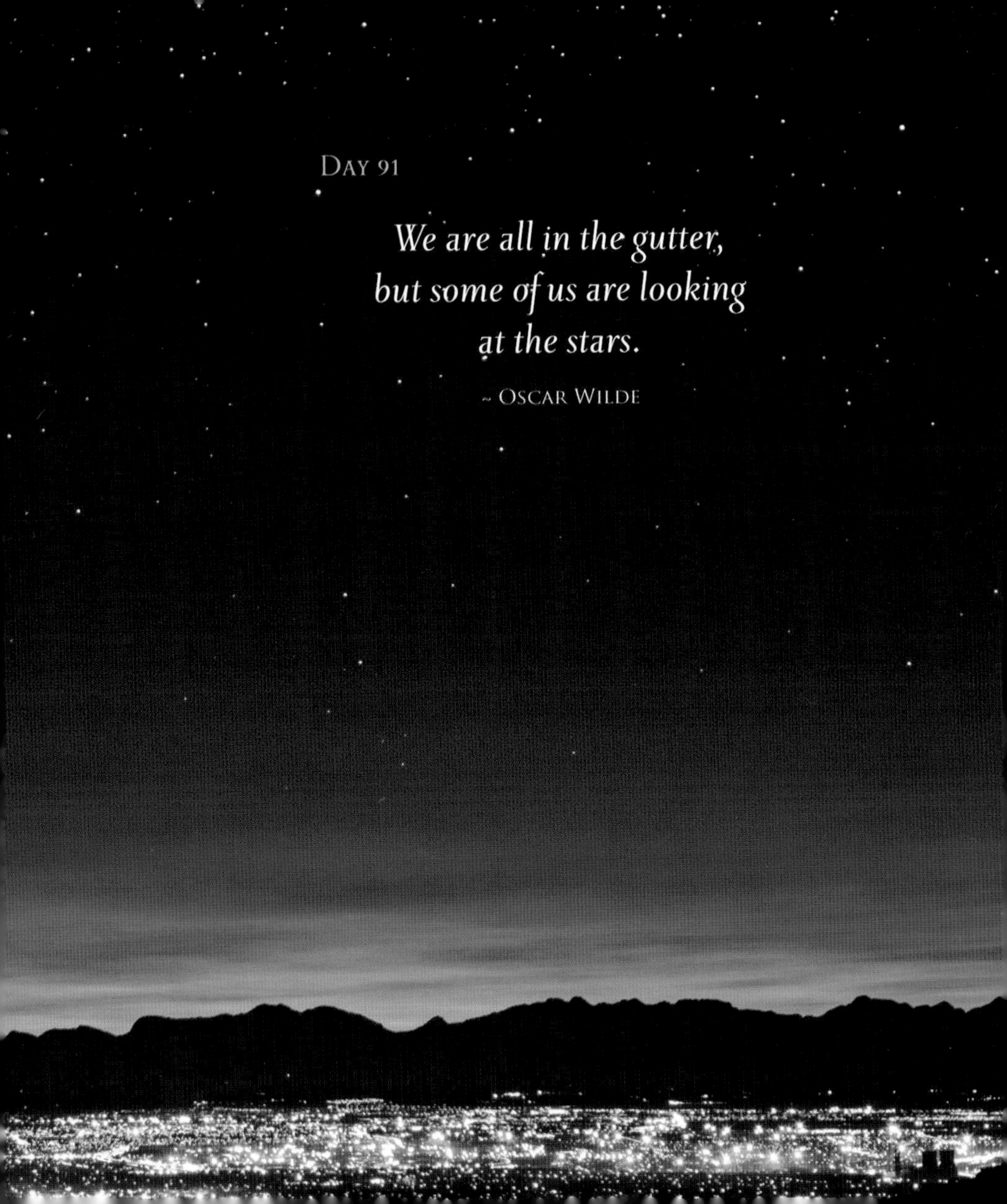

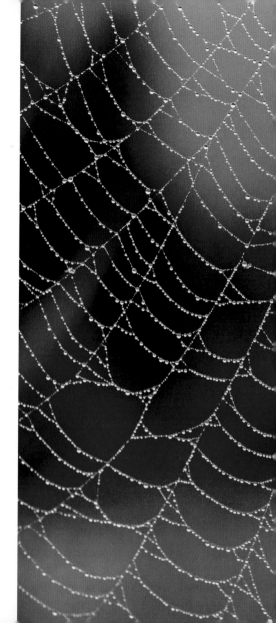

*Our thoughts,
our words, and deeds
are the threads of the
net which we throw
around ourselves.*

~ SWAMI VIVEKANANDA

We shall not cease from exploration
And the end of all our exploring
Will be to arrive where we started
And know the place for the first time.

~ T. S. ELIOT

One can never read the same book twice.

~ EDMUND WILSON

Drop by drop
is the pitcher filled.

~ BUDDHA

Patience is passion tamed.

~ Lyman Abbott

Diamonds are nothing more than
chunks of coal that stuck to their job.

~ MALCOLM FORBES

*Patience serves as a protection
against wrongs as clothes
do against cold.*

~ LEONARDO DA VINCI

*Nothing great is
produced suddenly.*

~ EPICTETUS

DAY 100

There are no stronger enemies
than patience and time.

~ LEO TOLSTOY

What wound did ever heal but by degrees?

~ WILLIAM SHAKESPEARE

DAY 102

You get to the point when there are things you enjoy that start getting hard—that's when you know you're getting good, and you have to stick through it.

~ MICHELLE OBAMA

Someone is sitting in the shade today because
someone planted a tree a long time ago.

~ WARREN BUFFETT

DAY 104

To drink in the spirit of a place you should be not only alone but not hurried.

~ GEORGE SANTAYANA

*Experience has taught me this:
that we undo ourselves by
impatience. Misfortunes have
their life and their limits, their
sickness and their health.*

~ MICHEL DE MONTAIGNE

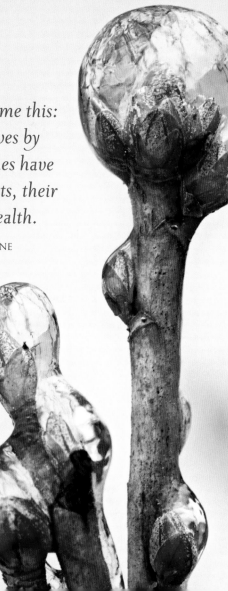

*Just when the caterpillar thought the
world was over, it became a butterfly.*

~ PROVERB

Learn to labor and to wait.

~ HENRY WADSWORTH LONGFELLOW

DAY 108

Little strokes fell great oaks.

~ BENJAMIN FRANKLIN

Perfection is attained by slow degrees;
she requires the hand of time.

~ VOLTAIRE

Trees slow of growth bear the best fruit.

~ MOLIÈRE

The best way out is always through.

~ ROBERT FROST

Rivers know this: there is no hurry.
We shall get there some day.

~ A. A. MILNE

*Satisfaction is quietness of heart
under the course of destiny.*

~ AL-HARITH AL-MUHASIBI

*Genius is only a greater aptitude
for patience.*

~ GEORGES-LOUIS LECLERC DE BUFFON

*It's not that I'm so smart,
it's just that I stay with
problems longer.*

~ ALBERT EINSTEIN

*Besides the noble art of getting things done,
there is a nobler art of leaving things undone.*

~ LIN YUTANG

*The best way to pay for a
lovely moment is to enjoy it.*

~ RICHARD BACH

*Anyone's life truly lived consists
of work, sunshine, exercise,
soap, plenty of fresh air,
and a happy contented spirit.*

~ LILLIE LANGTRY

DAY 119

The one at peace sleeps pleasantly,
having abandoned victory and defeat.

~ BUDDHA

To love what you do and feel that it matters—how could anything be more fun?

~ KATHARINE GRAHAM

Be grateful for luck. Pay the thunder no mind.
Listen to the birds. And don't hate nobody.

~ JAMES HUBERT "EUBIE" BLAKE

When you come right down to it,
the secret of having it all is loving it all.

~ JOYCE BROTHERS

The greater part of our happiness or misery depends on our dispositions, and not upon our circumstances.

~ MARTHA WASHINGTON

*I never found the companion that was
so companionable as solitude.*

~ HENRY DAVID THOREAU

Day 125

*I have perceived that
to be with those I like
is enough.*

~ WALT WHITMAN

DAY 126

*We are happy when
we are growing.*

~ W. B. YEATS

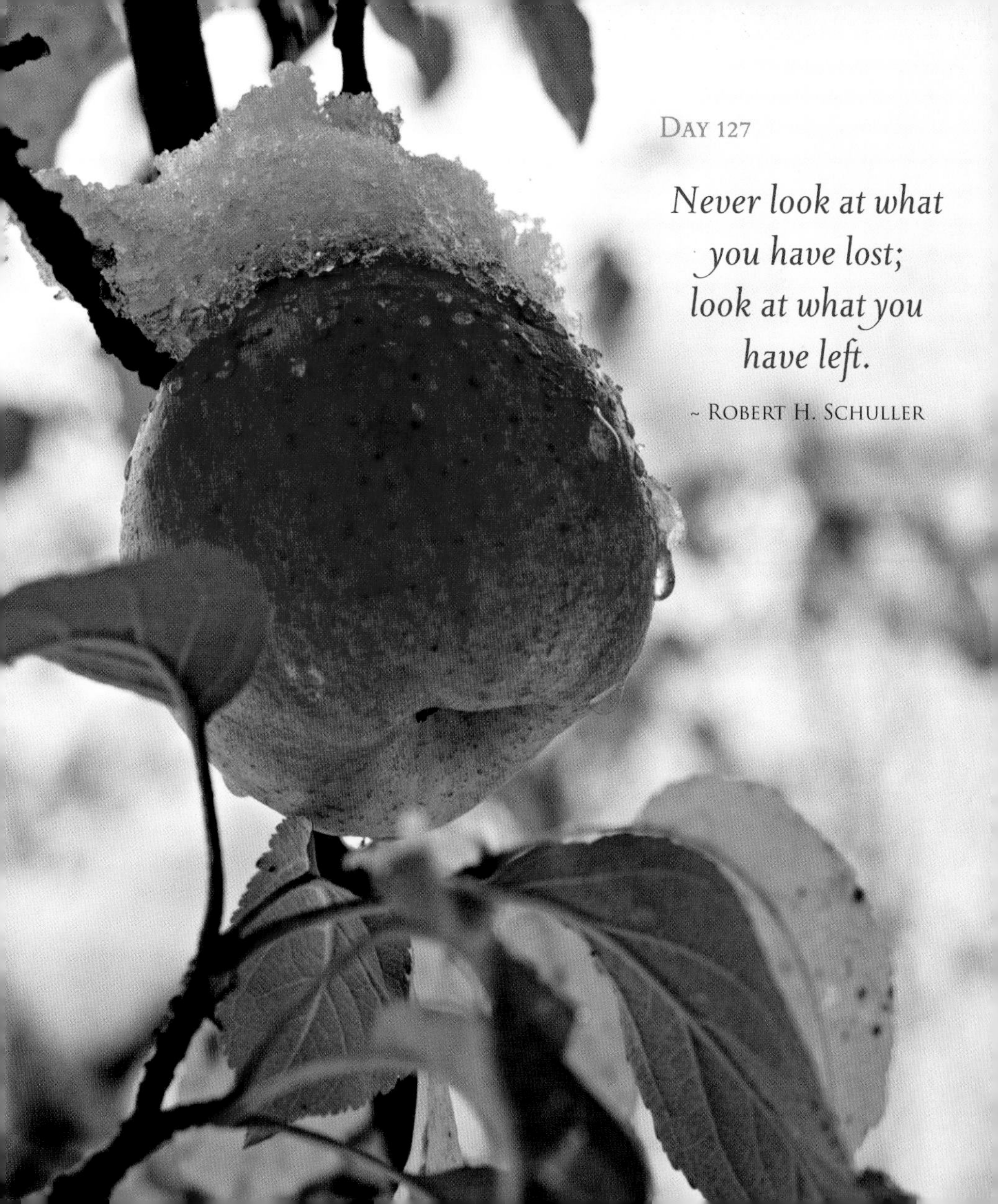

Day 127

Never look at what you have lost; look at what you have left.

~ Robert H. Schuller

DAY 128

Be content with what you have;
rejoice in the way things are.
When you realize there is nothing lacking,
the whole world belongs to you.

~ LAO-TZU

Taking a midday nap
feet planted
on a cool wall.

~ MATSUO BASHŌ

One joy scatters a hundred griefs.

~ CHINESE PROVERB

It is with life as it is with a play—
it matters not how long the action is
spun out, but how good the acting is.

~ LUCIUS ANNAEUS SENECA

One must view the world through the eye in one's heart rather than just trust the eyes in one's head.

~ MARY CROW DOG

DAY 133

The foolish man seeks happiness in the distance;
the wise grows it under his own feet.

~ JAMES OPPENHEIM

Fall seven times, stand up eight.

~ JAPANESE PROVERB

*A thousand words leave not
the same deep print as does a single deed.*

~ HENRIK IBSEN

Cease to be a drudge;
seek to be an artist.

~ MARY McLEOD BETHUNE

By three methods we may learn wisdom:
First, by reflection, which is noblest;
second, by imitation, which is easiest;
and third, by experience,
which is the bitterest.

~ CONFUCIUS

The first thing to do is fall in love
with your work.

~ PROVERB

Surviving is important,
but thriving is elegant.

~ MAYA ANGELOU

Long experience has taught me that to be criticized is not always to be wrong.

~ ANTHONY EDEN

Change will only come about when we become more forgiving, compassionate, loving, and above all joyful in the knowledge that we can change as those around us can change too.

~ MAIREAD MAGUIRE

Science is not only compatible with spirituality; it is a profound source of spirituality.

~ Carl Sagan

But one does not forget by trying to forget.
One only remembers.

~ RICHARD RODRIGUEZ

DAY 144

*The sea does not reward those who are
too anxious, too greedy, or too impatient.
One should lie empty, open, choiceless as a beach—
waiting for a gift from the sea.*

~ ANNE MORROW LINDBERGH

There are two ways of getting home.
One of them is to stay there;
the other is to walk round the whole
world till we come back to the same place.

~ G. K. CHESTERTON

You may have noticed that if one has money
without brains, he cannot use it to advantage;
but if one has brains without money, they will enable
him to live comfortably to the end of his days.

~ L. FRANK BAUM

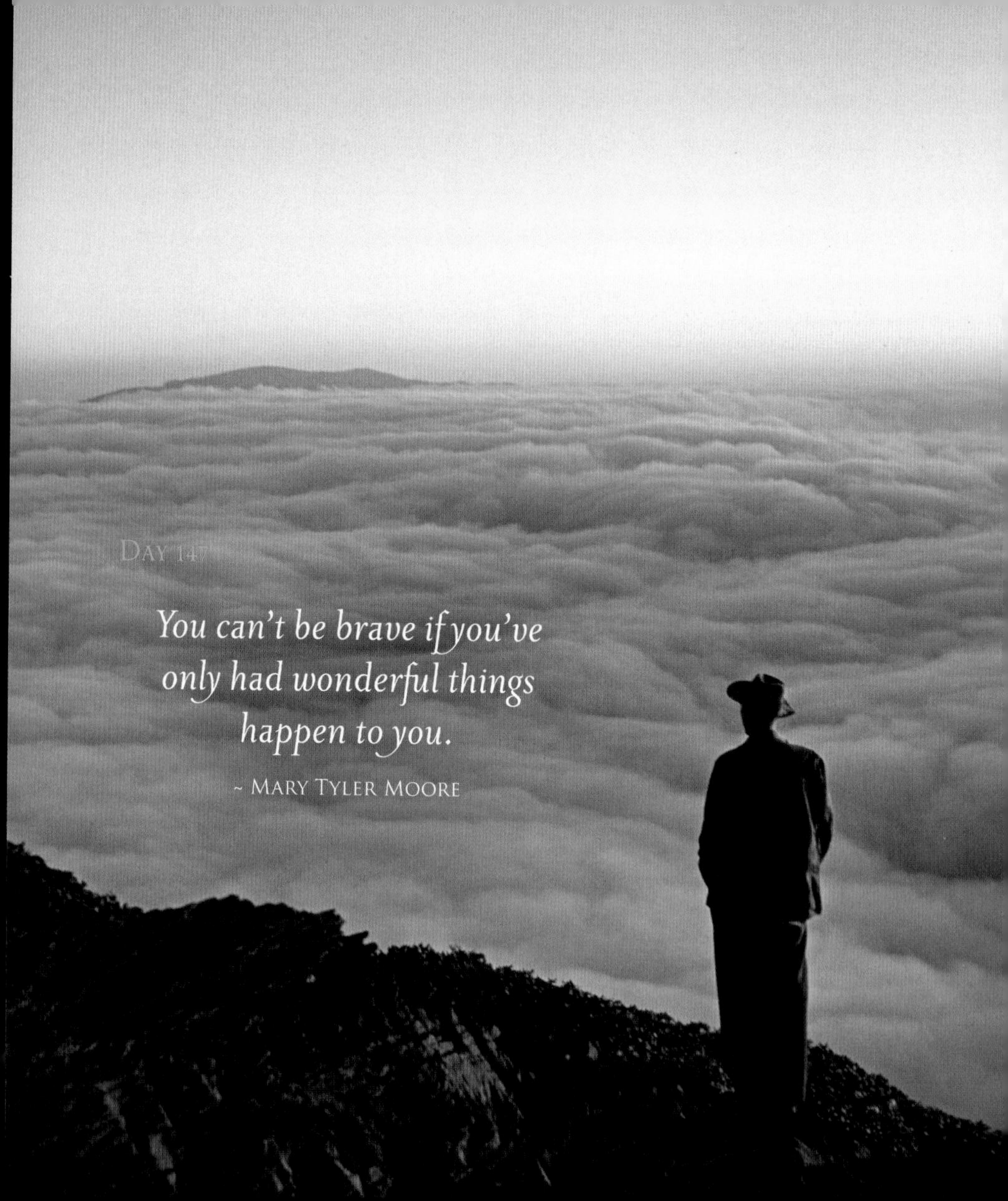

DAY 147

You can't be brave if you've only had wonderful things happen to you.

~ MARY TYLER MOORE

Trouble is part of your life.
If you don't share it, you don't give
the person who loves you a
chance to love you enough.

~ DINAH SHORE

DAY 149

If you rest, you rust.

~ HELEN HAYES

DAY 150

The secret of life and art is the threefold:
getting started, keeping going,
and getting started again.

~ SEAMUS HEANEY

Knowledge does not come to us by details, but in flashes of light from heaven.

~ HENRY DAVID THOREAU

DAY 152

Reflect on our present blessings
of which every man has many—
not on your past misfortunes,
of which all men have some.

~ CHARLES DICKENS

*We should not spoil what we have by
desiring what we do not have,
but remember that what we have too was
the gift of fortune.*

~ Epicurus

Silent gratitude isn't very much
to anyone.

~ GERTRUDE STEIN

DAY 155

*Walk as if you were kissing
the earth with your feet.*

~ THICH NHAT HANH

We can only be said to be alive in those moments when our hearts are conscious of our treasures.

~ Thornton Wilder

*I would maintain that thanks are the highest
form of thought; and that gratitude is
happiness doubled by wonder.*

~ G. K. CHESTERTON

*It's in the human spirit
to remember a giving hand.*

~ Audrey Hepburn

*Watch the stars, and see yourself
running with them.*

~ MARCUS AURELIUS

DAY 160

Rest and be thankful.

~ WILLIAM WORDSWORTH

When we lose one blessing, another is often most unexpectedly given in its place.

~ C. S. Lewis

*Every hour of the light
and dark is a miracle.*

~ WALT WHITMAN

It was only a sunny smile,
and little it cost in the giving;
but it scattered the night
Like morning light,
And made the day worth living.

~ TRADITIONAL AMERICAN POEM

DAY 164

The thankful receiver
bears a plentiful harvest.

~ WILLIAM BLAKE

*Gratitude is the memory
of the heart.*

~ JEAN BAPTISTE MASSIEU

DAY 166

There are times when we stop. We sit still . . .
We listen and breezes from a whole other world
begin to whisper.

~ JAMES CARROLL

DAY 167

*Our work for peace must begin
within the private world
of each one of us.*

~ Dag Hammarskjöld

Each dream finds a shape in the end;
there is a draught to quench every thirst,
and a love for every heart.

~ GUSTAVE FLAUBERT

DAY 169

It isn't enough to talk about peace;
one must believe in it.
And it isn't enough to believe in it;
one must work at it.

- ELEANOR ROOSEVELT

Now stir the fire, and close the shutters fast
Let fall the curtains, wheel the sofa round . . .
So let us welcome peaceful evening in.

~ WILLIAM COWPER

Water becomes clear through stillness.
How can I become still?
By flowing with the stream.

~ LAO-TZU

DAY 172

The house was quiet and the world was calm.
The reader became the book.

~ WALLACE STEVENS

I rest in the grace of the world,
and am free.

~ WENDELL BERRY

He has great tranquility of heart
who cares for neither
praise nor blame.

~ THOMAS À KEMPIS

DAY 175

*However vast the darkness,
we must supply our own light.*

~ STANLEY KUBRICK

Only the development of compassion and understanding for others can bring us the tranquility and happiness we all seek.

~ DALAI LAMA

DAY 177

Peace is not the absence of conflict,
but the ability to cope with conflict
by peaceful means.

- RONALD REAGAN

DAY 178

We place a happy life in a tranquility of mind.

~ CICERO

Go within every day and find the inner strength so that the world will not blow your candle out.

~ KATHERINE DUNHAM

To have darkness behind me,
in front of me a bright sky, flickering lights
on the water, and to feel
on the stony face the southern sun.

~ JULIA HARTWIG

Do your work, then step back.
The only path to serenity.

~ Lao-tzu

DAY 182

*None but ourselves
can free our minds.*

~ BOB MARLEY

CREDITS

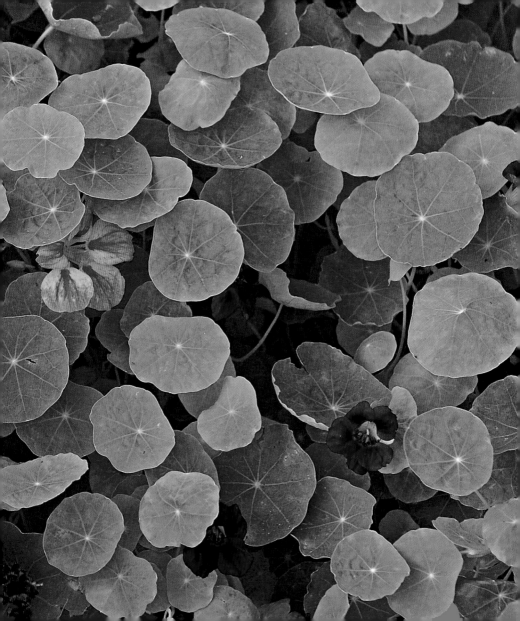

CONTRIBUTOR INDEX

Chesterton, G. K. (Gilbert Keith)
1874–1936
British journalist, playwright, philosopher, poet, and critic.

Chödrön, Pema (Deirdre Blomfield-Brown)
b. 1936
American teacher, author, and Tibetan Buddhist nun.

Churchill, Winston Spencer
1874–1965
British prime minister and statesman.

Cicero, Marcus Tullius
106–43 B.C.
Roman philosopher, statesman, and orator.

Coelho, Paulo
b. 1947
Brazilian novelist and lyricist.

Confucius
551–479 B.C.
Chinese philosopher and teacher.

Cousteau, Jacques-Yves
1910–1997
French author and oceanographer.

Cowper, William
1731–1800
English poet and hymnodist.

Crow Dog, Mary
1954–2013
Sicangu Lakota writer and activist.

Cunningham, Evelyn
1916–2010
American journalist.

D

Dalai Lama (Tenzin Gyatso)
b. 1935
Tibetan spiritual and political leader.

Dickens, Charles
1812–1870
English writer and social critic.

Disraeli, Benjamin
1804–1881
British prime minister.

Douglass, Frederick
1818–1895
American social reformer, writer, and orator.

Dunham, Katherine
1909–2006
American dancer, social activist, and author.

Dürer, Albrecht
1471–1528
German painter, mathematician, and theorist.

E

Ebner-Eschenbach, Marie von
1830–1916
Austrian writer.

Edelman, Marian Wright
b. 1939
American activist.

Eden, Anthony
1897–1977
British prime minister.

Einstein, Albert
1879–1955
German-American theoretical physicist.

Eliot, George (Mary Ann Evans)
1819–1880
British novelist.

Eliot, T. S. (Thomas Stearns)
1888–1965
British poet and playwright.

Epictetus
A.D. 55–135
Greek sage and Stoic philosopher.

Epicurus
341–269 B.C.
Greek philosopher.

F

Fisher, M. F. K. (Mary Frances Kennedy)
1908–1992
American food writer.

Flaubert, Gustave
1821–1880
French novelist.

Forbes, Malcolm
1919–1990
American businessman
and publisher.

Franklin, Benjamin
1706–1790
American inventor, author,
politician, diplomat, and
scientist.

Frost, Robert
1874–1963
American poet.

G

Gandhi, Mohandas
Karamchand (Mahatma)
1869–1948
Indian civil rights leader.

Gide, André Paul
Guillaume
1869–1947
French author.

Glass, Philip
b. 1937
American composer.

Goethe, Johann Wolfgang von
1749–1832
German novelist,
poet, playwright,
and philosopher.

Goldsmith, Joan Oliver
b. 1951
American author,
singer, and professional
speaker.

Goodall, Jane
b. 1934
British primatologist
and anthropologist.

Graham, Katharine
1917–2001
American publisher.

H

Hammarskjöld, Dag
1905–1961
Swedish diplomat,
economist, and author.

Hanh, Thich Nhat
b. 1926
Vietnamese Buddhist
monk, poet, author, and
activist.

Hartwig, Julia
b. 1921
Polish poet.

Hayes, Helen
1900–1993
American actress.

Heaney, Seamus
1939-2013
Irish poet.

Hepburn, Audrey
1929–1993
British actress and
humanitarian.

Hill, Napoleon
1883–1970
American author, lawyer,
and journalist.

I

Ibsen, Henrik
1828–1906
Norwegian playwright
and poet.

J

Jung, Carl (Gustav)
1875–1961
Swiss psychiatrist and
founder of analytical
psychology.

K

Keller, Helen
1880–1968
American writer, lecturer,
and activist.

Kennedy, John Fitzgerald
1917–1963
American President.

King, Martin Luther, Jr.
1929–1968
American clergyman,
activist, and leader.

Kubrick, Stanley
1928–1999
American film
director, producer,
and screenwriter.

L

L'Amour, Louis
1908–1988
American author.

Langtry, Lillie
1853–1929
British singer and actress.

Lao-tzu
604–531 B.C.
Chinese philosopher.

Leclerc de Buffon,
Georges-Louis
1707–1788
French naturalist,
cosmologist, and author.

Le Guin, Ursula K.
b. 1929
American novelist, poet,
and essayist.

Leonardo da Vinci
1452–1519
Italian artist, inventor,
and writer.

Lewis, C. S. (Clive Staples)
1898–1963
Irish novelist, scholar,
and broadcaster.

Lincoln, Abraham
1809–1865
American President.

Lindbergh, Anne Morrow
1906–2001
American writer, poet,
and aviator.

Lin Yutang
1895–1976
Chinese novelist, essayist,
and translator.

Longfellow, Henry
Wadsworth
1807–1882
American poet.

Loren, Sophia
b. 1934
Italian actress.

Luther, Martin
1483–1546
German monk, priest,
and professor.

M

Maguire, Mairead
b. 1944
Northern Irish peace
activist.

Marcus Aurelius
A.D. 121–180
Roman emperor.

Marley, Bob (Nesta
Robert)
1945–1981
Jamaican singer-
songwriter and musician.

Massieu, Jean Baptiste
1772–1846
French educator.

McCarthy, Mary
1912–1989
American author.

Mead, Margaret
1901–1978
American cultural
anthropologist.

Merton, Thomas
1915–1968
American writer.

Miller, Henry
1891–1980
American novelist.

Milne, A. A. (Alan
Alexander)
1882–1956
English novelist, poet,
and playwright.

Molière (Jean-Baptiste
Poquelin)
1622–1673
French playwright
and actor.

Montaigne, Michel de
1533–1592
French writer and
philosopher.

Moore, Mary Tyler
b. 1936
American actress.

Morris, William
1834–1896
English artist, writer,
and designer.

al-Muhasibi, al-Harith
781–857
Theologian and Sufi
teacher.

Mumford, Lewis
1895–1990
American historian,
philosopher, and literary
critic.

N

Norris, Kathleen
b. 1947
American poet
and essayist.

O

Obama, Michelle
b. 1964
American First Lady,
lawyer, and activist.

Oppenheim, James
1882–1932
American poet, novelist,
and editor.

P

Plath, Sylvia
1932–1963
American poet, novelist,
and short-story writer.

Pollan, Michael
b. 1955
American journalist,
author, and professor.

Porter, Katherine Anne
1890–1980
American journalist,
novelist, and political
activist.

R

Ramakrishna, Sri
1836–1886
Indian priest and spiritual
leader.

Reagan, Ronald
1911–2004
American President
and actor.

Reynolds, Sir Joshua
1723–1792
English painter.

Rich, Adrienne
1929–2012
American poet, essayist,
and feminist.

Robinson, Marilynne
b. 1943
American novelist
and essayist.

Rodriguez, Richard
b. 1944
American writer.

Roosevelt, (Anna) Eleanor
1884–1962
American First Lady,
activist, and author.

Rossetti, Christina
1830–1894
English poet.

Rousseau, Jean-Jacques
1712–1778
Swiss philosopher
and writer.

Rukeyser, Muriel
1913–1980
American poet and
political activist.

Rumi (Jalal ad-Din
ar-Rumi)
1207–1273
Persian poet.

S

Sagan, Carl
1934–1996
American astronomer,
astrophysicist, and author.

Santayana, George
1863–1952
Spanish-American
philosopher, poet,
and novelist.

Schuller, Robert Harold
b. 1926
American televangelist
and author.

Schweitzer, Albert
1875–1965
German and French
philosopher, musician,
and physician.

Seeger, Pete
1919-2014
American folk singer.

Shakespeare, William
1564–1616
British playwright
and poet.

Shore, Dinah
1916–1994
American singer and
actress.

Spencer, Diana
1961–1997
Wife of Charles, Prince of
Wales, and international
humanitarian.

Stein, Gertrude
1874–1946
American novelist
and poet.

Stevens, Wallace
1879–1955
American Modernist
poet.

Szymborska, Wisława
1923–2012
Polish poet and essayist.

T
Teale, Edwin Way
1899–1980
American naturalist,
writer, and photographer.

Thomas à Kempis
1380–1471
Dutch priest, monk,
and writer.

Thoreau, Henry David
1817–1862
American author, poet,
and philosopher.

Tolkien, J. R. R. (John
Ronald Reuel)
1892–1973
English writer, poet,
and professor.

Tolstoy, Leo
1828–1910
Russian novelist and
short-story writer.

U
Updike, John
1932–2009
American novelist, poet,
and critic.

V
Vivekananda, Swami
(Narendra Nath Datta)
1863–1902
Indian Hindu monk.

Voltaire (François-Marie
Arouet)
1694–1778
French writer, playwright,
and philosopher.

Vonnegut, Kurt, Jr.
1922–2007
American writer.

W
Washington, George
1732–1799
American President.

Washington, Martha
1731–1802
American First Lady.

White, E. B. (Elwyn
Brooks)
1899–1985
American writer.

Whitman, Walt
1819–1892
American poet, essayist,
and journalist.

Whittier, John Greenleaf
1807–1892
American Quaker poet.

Wilde, Oscar
1854–1900
Irish novelist and
dramatist.

Wilder, Laura Ingalls
1867–1957
American author.

Wilder, Thornton
1897–1975
American playwright
and novelist.

Wilson, Edmund
1895–1972
American writer.

Wordsworth, William
1770–1850
English poet.

ILLUSTRATIONS CREDITS

If you have enjoyed this book
or it has touched your life in some way,
we would love to hear from you.

Please send your comments to:
Hallmark Book Feedback
P.O. Box 419034
Mail Drop 100
Kansas City, MO 64141

Or e-mail us at:
booknotes@hallmark.com